FAMOUS RAILWAY PHOTOGRAPHERS

P. RANSOME-WALLIS

This photograph was taken in 1955, from the footplate of a Class N-2 Tank locomotive en route for Hertford as it was overtaken at the entrance to Copenhagen Tunnel by a Class A-1 Pacific on the Flying Scotsman. It reminds me always of the noise, dirt, discomfort and thrills of footplate travel.

FAMOUS RAILWAY PHOTOGRAPHERS

P. RANSOME-WALLIS

DAVID & CHARLES
NEWTON ABBOT

0 7153 6233 X

Printed in Great Britain
by W J Holman Dawlish Devon
for David & Charles (Holdings) Limited
South Devon House Newton Abbot Devon

INTRODUCTION

Probably a child psychologist could find some interesting (and, perhaps, Freudian) reason for the fact that my earliest childhood memory is, not of my home or of my well-loved parents, but of a Great Central locomotive seen from the lower steps of a footbridge as it left Worksop station. I still remember the driver turning the reverser as he 'notched up' and saying, excitedly, to my mother: 'Look, he's steering the train!'

So began my life-long love of railway engines and, of course, there would never be any job for me other than that of a locomotive mechanical engineer.

Alas for my ambitions! In 1923, a year before I had planned to start as a pupil at Doncaster, the railways amalgamated into four groups and this greatly reduced the chances for promotion to the top jobs.

Acting on advice from friends in railway service, my father decided that I should, instead, follow the medical tradition of our family. So I found myself as the only undergraduate at the University of Edinburgh ever to have been admitted to the Faculty of Medicine by passing the entrance examination in the advanced grades of mathematics, mechanics, hydrostatics and physics!

During an immensely exciting and happy university career, my love of railways was never subdued and while still a medical student, I was giving lectures on valve gears and poppet valves to the LNER Mutual Improvement Classes at Haymarket and St Margarets locomotive depots.

After qualifying, the choice of hospital appointments and temporary work in general practice, was always influenced by the railway interest in the particular locality. Thus it was that, for

5

nearly two years, I worked in Swindon and had the privilege of meeting (only once) J.G. Churchward. In Swindon began several life-long friendships with railwaymen of which the most cherished and respected were those of the late (Sir) W. A. Stanier and his son, Bill. It was largely through Stanier's introductions that, in later years, so many privileges were obtained on railways all over the world. I remember, with great pride that, shortly before he died and despite the disability caused by a recent stroke, Stanier came to London to chair a (very poor) lecture which I gave to the Retired Railway Officers Association.

I came to Herne Bay, originally, for three months, the railway interest being the great diversity of motive power working on the Kent Coast Line of the Southern at that time. However, other 'forces' then began to take charge and in early 1934, I married my long-suffering fiancée, also a doctor of medicine, and entered into a happy medical partnership with my erstwhile employers.

My interest in locomotives has always been technical rather than emotional. While the beauty of a well balanced design was certainly appreciated, the colour of the paint or the number the engine carried meant very little and I never 'collected numbers' — official lists could usually be obtained for the asking. Numbers which *were* remembered were those of engines which had some unusual structural or mechanical interest. For example, the *GN* small Atlantic, No 983 had outside bogie frames, why, I have never discovered, and the Raven Pacific No 2401 was the only British locomotive which had a Westinghouse combined ejector instead of the usual Gresham and Craven 'Dreadnought'.

From an early age, my major interest has been in continental and overseas motive power and, in 1929, a motor-cycle tour through seven countries to Budapest, opened up a vast and exciting new field of study. The simple little British 4-4-0s and 4-6-0s were insignificant when compared with the great machines of Austria, Germany and France. From that time, a year has never passed without a visit to at least one foreign country to see its railways.

World War II kept me away from my home for six and a half years. As a Naval Reservist I was mobilised before the outbreak and not released until some months after VJ day. During the war, I was frequently scared stiff but never bored and it was by far the most interesting and instructive period of my life.

Service with the Royal Navy provided wonderful opportunities for travel and, armed with W. A. Stanier's introductory card, I was accepted by railwaymen in many parts of Africa, Asia and America and given most generous hospitality and privileges. Above all, I was able to see quite a lot of the British Empire and to be justly very proud of what I saw.

Two long spells of duty in the United States and Canada, the first before the Americans were at war, provided time to see and to travel on many of the world's greatest locomotives and also to 'clock' my first 100 mph on a diesel locomotive. I visited the ALCO Plant at Schenectady, NY, when Union Pacific 'Big Boys' were carrying out trials. Steam tests were also being carried out on one of the huge boilers for these engines and, to stand beneath the firebox while oil-burners above raised the pressure to blowing-off point, was awe-inspiring.

How amazing it was that these great, sophisticated Mallet simples were direct descendants of the little narrow-gauge 4-cylinder compounds first designed in 1884 by Anatole Mallet for use on lightly laid track with severe curvature and steep gradients.

The war ended at last and then came the tremendous task of making a living from an area which had evacuated about 50 per cent of its population. By dint of working more hours than were ever dreamt of by trade unions, things gradually became less grim and, by 1948, our pre-war standards were almost attained. Then, on 5 July of that fateful year, the introduction of the National Health Service at a stroke cut my income by nearly 40 per cent. To try to offset some of this loss, I started to write and, by working far into every night, article followed article and book followed book. Railways provided most of the subjects but the Royal Navy, anti-submarine warfare, ships and the sea all helped to finance the education of my two girls and to provide for family holidays and my journeys abroad to obtain new material and photographs.

During those strenuous years, my wife often acted as my unpaid deputy as, for example, in 1955 when I travelled nearly 7,000 miles on footplates in Britain and France to obtain material for yet another book. All of it pretty hard going but not without much interest and a lot of fun particularly with the French enginemen who, without exception, are the most skilled and the most humorous railwaymen I know.

The years 1960 and 1961 were the most interesting of the postwar era. One morning, the phone rang and a strange voice asked me to hold the line for a Mr Richard Keen of the BBC. It transpired that a certain Mr Douglas Brown was to have broadcast in a programme called 'On Railways' but could not do so. Would I like to do the job? I said I would and, the following day, went to Portland Place to see what was involved. I was to take a tape recorder down to Wellingborough and, next morning, to travel on a BR Class 9 freight locomotive working a coal train from there to Brent Yard. I was to record the noises of the locomotive and my own running commentary. It all went surprisingly well and, in due course, I listened to the broadcast in the comfort of my own home.

Thus began a most happy and profitable relationship with the 'On Railways' team and, during the next two years, I was 'the man from the BBC' on the railways of France, Spain, Germany, Italy and Finland, as well as on several assignments in Britain. Most of the work was done from the footplate and I carried with me a large and heavy tape recorder; the transistorised instruments were then still in their infancy. Largely because of the increasing use of diesel and electric locomotives, neither of which produces interesting noises, the programme came to an end and my broadcasting days were over.

The railways of the Communist countries of Eastern Europe were known to have many of the most interesting and advanced locomotives in Europe. Inspired, I think, by the audacious journeys made by my friend A. E. (Dusty) Durrant, I rather timidly made some journeys by car to Czechoslovakia, East Germany and Poland. They were not very successful; only rarely was permission given to visit locomotive depots and photography of trains and engines had to be carried out from 'hides' in the country or during the lunch-hour at stations, (even the *Gestapo* have to eat!) Once, a Czech driver heaved a lump of coal at me as I photographed his train and I was arrested several times, though only once, in Poland, was my film confiscated.

It appeared that 'the game was not worth the candle'. Later regulations were eased and parties of railway enthusiasts made visits behind the Iron Curtain. So I visited all the Communist countries except Russia, Rumania and Albania with parties from one or other of the railway societies to which I belong. Even so, nearly always, some local *gauleiter*, jealous of his authority has prevented our making some scheduled visits to works or depots.

The change of Government in 1964 brought with it vast financial improvements for my profession and, at last, I am no longer dependent upon my literary and photographic efforts to live graciously. So this book may well be my swan-song, and in it I have chosen photographs taken on railways at home and abroad during the last fifty years. Many have been published before, both here and overseas. I make no apology for including them as I have selected those which I think are of the greatest interest. My own interest in rack systems and in articulated locomotives is evident in my selection and I have included a section to show some of the streamline forms adopted, often unwillingly, by locomotive engineers of the twenties and thirties.

Nostalgic memories of adventures with steam will never be forgotten but always to look back is profitless and stultifying. Modern forms of motive power, are of great interest — particularly electric traction — even though the technicalities present a great challenge to one's ageing brain. But I happily accept that challenge.

Photography of locomotives and trains has always been a means to an end whereby illustrations of the machines in which I was interested could be made, studied at leisure and filed to make a comprehensive and permanent record.

I started railway photography in 1917 when I was given a No 2 Box Brownie camera and, having loaded it with Kodak non-curling film, I sallied forth to take my first railway photograph, a Great Central train near Shireoaks. It came out remarkably well, has often been published and the negative is as good now as on the day it was made.

Later I decided to try to obtain photographs of one of every class of British locomotives taking a '¾-front' view of one side of the engine and tender and a '¾-rear' view of the other side, engine only. I also wanted a clear picture of each class on a train.

The object was to make good record photographs; clouds of smoke and steam were not essential or even desirable. Neither were pictorial locations and, with a clear, unconfused background, it did not matter if many exposures were made from the same spot. I tried to emulate the late F. E. Mackay, one of the greatest railway photographers.

I never achieved my object though I came very near to doing so.

Good record photographs of locomotives should be free from such intrusions as poles and posts and when these cannot be avoided they must be 'blocked out'. 'Blocking out' on the negative leaves a white 'ghost' on the print which can be removed (or converted into a cloud!) by careful application of that most useful, but highly poisonous, iodo-cyanide reducer which can also be used to increase print contrast and to bring out detail in areas of deep shadow.

I classify railway photographs as record, pictorial-record and pictorial. When, in 1948, I had to 'go commercial', many previous standards had to be jettisoned as most editors just love clouds of steam and smoke, bits of foliage and 'arty' locations. But I still think that a good record photograph is the most worthwhile, though amateurs find it most difficult to achieve.

My first photographs were published in the *Railway Magazine* in January 1925 and, since then, a very large number has been reproduced all over the world. There is nothing more satisfying than to have a good print well produced; there is nothing more frustrating than to have a good print badly reproduced.

I have always given priority to monochrome photography though I have about 1500 colour transparencies of railway subjects, all in the 6 x 6cm or 6 x 9cm formats. They make a very pleasant showing and evoke far more emotion in many viewers than do monochrome prints.

My first visit to Portugal was in 1937 when the ship in which I was serving spent several days at Lisbon. At that time, the Portuguese Railway Company (CP) owned half the railways and operated the more important State-owned lines among which was the Sul e Sueste (SS) whose territory was south and south-east of the Tagus. Its headquarters were at Barreiro, across the river from Lisbon.

The SS owned an interesting assortment of ancient locomotives and had, but recently, retired the 1862 Beyer Peacock single wheeler *D. Luiz*. One of the old engines I found at Barreiro was the 0-4-2 illustrated here. No 1008 was built by Beyer Peacock in 1863 and had been modernised, only by the provision of a sand-box on top of the boiler. It was still at work on local passenger trains and I enjoyed a short trip on its footplate.

Still at work on the 1067mm (3ft 6in) gauge Indonesian State Railways (PNKA) is a number of these outside cylinder 2-4-0s which were built by Sharp Stewart in 1880. No B50 06 was photographed at Madiun in 1970. It is seen drawn up beside the log bin after having its tender filled with wood fuel. Most of these 2-4-0s are wood burners and so the brick arch in the firebox has been removed. They are used for light branch-line trains and for duties as shed pilots.

Photographed leaving Market Harborough with a train from Peterborough to Nottingham in 1938, was this old London Midland & Scottish Railway 2-4-0 No 20002.

Originally belonging to the No 1 Class of the Midland Railway, this ancient double-framed locomotive was outshopped by Derby Works in 1866. By 1938, however, little of the original machine remained as it had been completely rebuilt at least twice and had received new cylinders and new boilers.

The Salter safety valves on the dome were much in evidence on old Midland engines as they were on contemporary machines on the Continent. It would be of interest to know on which railway they were first used.

To work over their predominantly level tracks, the Danish State Railways (DSB) never required locomotives of great power. Until the post-war acquisition of Class 52 German 2-10-0s, a series of 3-cylinder 2-8-0s were the most powerful freight locomotives. For express passenger duties, maximum power was provided by the Class E, 4-cylinder, balanced compound Pacifics of which eleven were bought from Sweden in 1936 after electrification had made them redundant and twenty-five more were built for DSB by Frichs in 1943-7.

Until complete dieselisation, however, local DSB passenger traffic was worked by small and often ancient, locomotives such as this 4-4-0 No 566 of Class K-2 which was photographed at Dybbolsbro in 1954. One hundred 4-4-0s of Class K were built during 1894-1904 and many were rebuilt as Class K-2 with superheaters and piston valves, during 1925-32. The outside Allan link motion was retained.

Photographed at Newbury, NH, in 1941 while working a train from Claremont Junction to Concord, was this old 4-4-0 of the Boston and Maine Railroad. No 1025 of Class A-41-F was hand-fired and was not superheated. The flat slide valves above the cylinders were operated, through rocking shafts, by Stephenson link motion inside the frames.

The consist of this branch line train was entirely of old clerestory stock and the whole scene might well have come from 1910, the year in which No 1025 was outshopped. The train is seen crossing the highway on a grade crossing and above the station building are the twin semaphores of the train-order signal.

While working in Dublin in 1929, I saw much of the Irish railways. The
mechanical engineers of all the companies generously provided facilities
and engine passes, many of which were renewed on my subsequent visits
before World War II.

The enormous variety and antiquity of so much of the locomotive
stock in the South made each visit full of interest but it required the
detailed classification sheets prepared by Inchicore Works to sort out
what was what and what it had been!

The Midland & Great Western was the second largest of the four
companies which, in 1925, amalgamated to form the Great Southern
Railways of which the standard gauge was 1600mm (5ft 3in). In 1939,
I photographed No 44, an ex MGW 4-4-0 as it ambled along the quay-
side at Wexford with a train for Rosslare. Classified D-19 by GSR,
No 44 was designed by McDonnell and built in 1877.

In the days before World War II, the Netherlands Railways (NS) were renowned for the beautiful appearance of their steam locomotives, which were painted apple-green with brown frames and had polished brass domes. There was a close association between the railways of Holland and the locomotive builders, Beyer Peacock of Manchester, England, who supplied many elegant double-framed 2-4-0s and 4-4-0s,

During 1932, I was given the 'freedom of the footplate' on the NS and I rode on many different classes. The saturated 4-4-0s of Class P^3 were wonderfully quiet and comfortable engines although the trains they worked over the mostly level terrain, were never very heavy.

My photograph shows a train from Amersfoort near Rotterdam (Maas) in charge of No 1758 (built BP 1901). Between 1889 and 1907, Beyer Peacock and Werkspoor built 137 of these little engines, some of which were, later, superheated.

The exhaust was invisible in the midday heat, dust and sand partially obscured the train and an Arab boy stopped begging and covered his ears with his hands as Egyptian State Railways 4-4-2 No 28 rushed by Rassoua with an express from Cairo to Port Said in 1940. Next day found me on the footplate of another of these fine old engines working the same train along the banks of the Suez Canal from Ismailiya to Port Said: and my Captain said: 'What peculiar things you do, Doc, when you go ashore'.

There were eighty of these very beautiful ESR Atlantics; the first five were built in Germany in 1913 and subsequent larger engines, with more grate area, came from Baldwin in 1921 and from German and British builders in 1925-6. For thirty years they worked the principal Egyptian express trains and many burned oil fuel (mazout). Two were rebuilt to 4-6-0 in 1933 and 1934 respectively.

J. G. Robinson's Atlantics for the Great Central Railway were among the most beautiful locomotives in Britain. Thirty-one came into LNER stock in 1923 of which four were 3-cylinder Smith compounds of Class 8D (LNE Class C-5) built 1905-6.

In appearance the two classes were similar but the compounds had one high pressure cylinder between the frames and two low pressure cylinders outside. Three sets of Stephenson link motion drove a piston valve for the high pressure and two slide valves for the low pressure cylinders respectively.

The performance of the GC Atlantics was greatly improved by super-heaters but was overshadowed in later years by the Director Class 4-4-0s which were much better engines.

Near Woodhouse in 1934, I photographed LNE No 5259 *King Edward VII*, Class C-5 with a Lincoln-Sheffield train of clerestory coaches. The Gresley 'flower-pot' was a cheaper substitute for Robinson's elegantly curvaceous chimney.

The extraordinary appearance of the inside-cylinder, streamline Atlantics of the Belgian National Railways (SNCB) is emphasised by this view of No 12.003 taken at Ostend in 1946.

Six of these Class 12 locomotives, with bar frames and 82¾in coupled wheels went into service in 1939, shortly before the outbreak of war. Their streamline casings successfully provided the best possible accessibility to working parts. The first four engines had piston valves, the last two, poppet valves.

They were designed to work fast, light trains between Brussels and Ostend — 72 miles in 60 minutes, start to stop. This they easily did but not without causing some excitement and trepidation in those privileged amateurs who rode on their very lively footplates!

After the war, they worked mainly between Brussels and Lille but there is no record of their achieving their designed maximum 90mph on those services.

In 1936 the Canadian Pacific Railway built five unusual 4-4-4 stream-line locomotives with 80in Boxpok type coupled wheels for working light-weight high speed inter-city trains These engines of Class F-2a had an unusually long wheelbase and the drive was to the leading coupled axle. Known as the Jubilee class they were unsatisfactory vehicles at high speeds though one of them holds the speed record for a steam locomotive in Canada, 120.4mph. In 1937 the first of a series of twenty locomotives appeared with a shorter wheelbase, and with the drive to the second pair of conventional-type 75in coupled wheels.

This series, of which No 2926 is shown here, was more successful but the whole project never really got off the ground and the loco-motives spent most of their time in normal passenger service. In both classes the boiler pressure was 300psi and originally a streamline casing enclosed the chimney. No 2926 was photographed in 1941 at Toronto, Ontario.

Until quite recently, scenes like the one shown here were commonplace on the 1675mm (5ft 5 15/16in)-gauge, Spanish National Railways System (RENFE) which had in service a great variety of the oldest 0-6-0s in the world.

My photograph was taken at Malaga in 1964. On the left, at the head of a long train of modern empty stock, is the Malaga station pilot, No 030-2495 built by Fives-Lille in 1892 for the Andalucian Railway. On an adjoining track, hauling a dirt train, is No 030-2352 which was built for the Madrid, Zaragoza and Alicante Railway in 1879.

A common sight on the railways of Britain, not so very long ago, was the 'pick-up goods'. Ambling gently along through the countryside, it stopped at all stations and sidings to exchange wagons and vans containing almost every form of merchandise.

The inside-cylinder 0-6-0 locomotive will forever be associated with these local freight workings and the single lamp over the left buffer was their well-known head code.

A rather powerful engine for the job was British Railways No 57667, an ex Caledonian superheated 0-6-0, designed by Pickersgill and introduced in 1918. It was shunting its train in Ballachulish goods yard prior to working back over the Connel Ferry Bridge to Oban. The neat little signal box was typical of many on the Caledonian Railway.

Western Australian Government Railways operate an extensive 1067mm (3ft 6in)-gauge system and, in 1970, their motive power depot at Bunbury, south of Perth, was one of the last steam strongholds in Australia. Seven different classes were allocated there, including two old locomotives still on the active list but used mainly to work special trains for railway enthusiasts. One was a 4-6-0, No 123 of Class G, built by Dübs in 1897. The other was this little 2-6-0, also Class G, which was the survivor of a series built by Martin between 1894 and 1898. It was in steam when I photographed it in 1970. The cone-topped vertical cylinder in front of the cab is the silencer for the vacuum brake ejector. While not seen in UK, this device was common on those Continental locomotives which used the vacuum brake.

A southbound freight train of the metre-gauge State Railway of Thailand was photographed in 1970 as it left the Bridge over the River Kwae Yai on its journey from Nam Tok to Kanchanaburi. The locomotive was 2-6-0, Class C-56 No 713 which was one of forty-two built in Japan during 1946-8.

The present bridge was completed by the Japanese in 1945 and has sixteen steel spans, ten of which originally were brought from dismantled bridges in Java. Allied bombing destroyed three of these spans in 1946 and the bridge was not reopened until 1952 after much reconstruction.

Near to the bridge, at Kanchanaburi, is the British and Allied War Cemetery. Quietly impressive and beautifully tended, this contains the graves of 6,844 of the men, 3,465 of them British who died while, as prisoners of war, they built the railway into Burma.

During 1951-4, the Polish State Railways (PKP) put into service 116 large mixed traffic 2-6-2 locomotives intended to replace the many old German locomotives working in Poland, especially the 4-6-0s of the Prussian Class P8.

The new engines were built by Chrzanow and were only slightly modified versions of the Russian 2-6-2s of Class Su(Cy). They have two simple cylinders and all have the ugly standard smoke deflectors of the PKP. They are hand-fired coal burners with welded boilers and three firebox arch tubes.

Class OL 49 No 109 was photographed at Poznan in 1965.

Photographed in 1957 leaving Venice, Mestre, with a train for Portogruaro, was this 4-cylinder 2-6-2 No 685.962 of the Italian State Railways (FS).

The Italians had few steam locomotives of any merit and the best were probably the 4-cylinder 2-6-2s of Group 685 which were put into service between 1912 and 1927. Many were rebuilds of saturated (and some superheated) Plancher compounds, some had piston valves and others Caprotti valves. All had Italian trucks and rode very smoothly in consequence.

No 685.962 was one of thirty engines of the last (1926-7) batch, all of which had Caprotti valves and five of which had Franco-Crosti pre-heaters (page 48) and were streamlined.

In 1941, when I spent some time on the Central Railroad of New Jersey, many of the Company's 'camel-back' locomotives were still in service, 0-6-0s, 0-8-0s and 4-6-0s, the last being extensively used on commuter trains from Jersey City Terminal.

The 'camel-back' or 'Mother Hubbard' locomotive, with the driver's cab outside the boiler, was the result of the adoption of the wide, anthracite-burning Wootton firebox first introduced on the Reading Railroad in 1880. This location of the cab was necessary to keep the structure within the loading gauge, but it also allowed more room on the narrow and often dangerous footplate for the fireman to feed the fire through two and sometimes three, fireholes.

My photograph taken at Communipaw, NJ shows No 629 of Class L-4-s built at ALCO's Brooks Works in 1904.

Delaware, Lackawanna and Western 4-6-0 No 1010 Class 8 was working a local train from Hoboken to Branchville, NJ, when it was photographed in 1941 at Wharton, NJ. The Class 8 engines were built originally as 'camel backs' and their appearance then resembled that of the New Jersey engine above. Despite the wide Wootton firebox with its two fireholes, the conventional cab was easily accommodated within the loading gauge when the engines were rebuilt.

Although the train is seen at a station, there are no platforms and passengers and their baggage cross the tracks to reach the station buildings. The DL & W is now amalgamated with the Erie RR and the 'Erie Lackawanna', is largely a freight system. Wharton no longer has a passenger station.

Blasting its way out of the docks complex at Port Elizabeth, Cape, with a heavy freight for the Classification Yards, was South African Railways 4-6-0 Class 6 No 439.

This was one of forty highly successful and reliable locomotives built by Dübs in 1893-4 for the Cape Government Railways and of which many were still in active service in 1968 when the photograph was taken. A large number of similar locomotives followed and, on SAR, these were sub-classes indicated by a capital letter after the numeral (6A, 6B etc). No 439 was virtually in its original form with a saturated Belpaire boiler and slide valves above the cylinders. Its only concession to modernity was the electric headlight.

The 1524mm (5ft 0in)-gauge Finnish State Railways (VR) had seven classes of 4-6-0 locomotives.

Drifting down past Pasila with a train from Mikkeli to Helsinki, in 1961, was No 785 of Class Hv 3. Twenty-four engines of this class were built during the twenty-one years 1921-41. They were comfortable engines on which to ride and, with a maximum axle-load of only 12.8 tonnes they had a high route availability. No 785 burned coal but some of the class were wood burners and in these, the brick arch was removed from the firebox.

Many steam locomotives of VR were fitted with piston by-pass valves which equalised pressure on each side of the piston when steam was shut off. Such a valve can clearly be seen protruding below the piston steam distribution valve on No 785.

During a short visit to India in 1940 I was able to visit several locomotive sheds and also to see one of India's famous named trains — The Flying Ranee of the Bombay Baroda & Central India Railway. This train ran the 163 miles between Bombay and Surat in 4hr 20min in each direction, with seven intermediate stops. The locomotives were Class H 4-6-0s and my photograph shows No 347, decorated and immaculate, leaving Bombay Central Station with the train.

The BBCI Class H 4-6-0s were built in six batches between 1908 and 1923. They were a British Engineering Standard type of which similar engines were built for other Indian railways. Engines built before 1909 were saturated with piston valves but were all later superheated and fifteen of them, including No 347, were given r.c. poppet valves.

No 01.1064, a rebuilt, oil-fired Pacific of the German Federal Railway (DB) was photographed with a train from Hamburg to Osnabruck as it started from a signal stop near Harburg in 1961.

The first of the 3-cylinder 4-6-2s of Class 01^{10} was streamlined and went into service in 1939. A further fifty-four of the class were built, without streamlining, in 1940.

In 1951, DB began an extensive programme of rebuilding many of the former Reichsbahn standard types (*Einheitslokomotiven*). The engines of Class 01^{10} which were rebuilt, received larger, welded boilers and most were oil-fired. They retained their single blastpipes but the auxiliaries (pumps etc) exhausted through the large diameter chimney casings. Roller bearings were provided for all axles and for the side rods and valve gear. Class 01^{10} had large and comfortable cabs and a deep throated exhaust beat which matched their massive appearance.

C

In 1940 I was in the Federated Malay States and made several footplate journeys on the metre-gauge FMSR locomotives. The most memorable was with the Day Mail from Kuala Lumpur to Singapore — 246 miles in 8hr 51min with 32 stops. The locomotive, throughout, was 3-cylinder Class 0-1 Pacific No 71 *Kuala Lumpur* fitted, as were all twenty-eight engines of the class, with r.c. poppet valves. The train was nine bogies including an air-conditioned dining car. The engine crew was changed three times; each crew consisted of a Scottish-named Anglo-Indian driver and two Malay firemen. All were pleasant and good railwaymen and I was allowed to drive for fifty miles. I also took a turn firing and thus had a most strenuous but happy day in the heat of a Malay summer.

My photograph shows the train on the passing loop at Kluang with the engine taking water.

Steaming across a level crossing (grade crossing) with an express from Bloemfontein, Orange Free State, to Kimberley, Cape, in 1968, was South African Railways 4-6-2 No 854 Class 16E. Six of these locomotives were built by Henschel in 1935 and their 72in coupled wheels were the largest ever to be fitted to a 1067mm (3ft 6in)-gauge locomotive. The two outside cylinders had r.c. poppet valves and the wide firebox had five arch tubes and a grate area of 63sq ft.

These locomotives were built to work the Union Limited Express (Johannesburg-Cape Town) and it was (unofficially) stated that they were the first 1067mm-gauge steam locomotives to achieve a speed of over 60mph.

During my stay in Bloemfontein in 1941, I rode on No 855 and a speed in excess of that figure was held for several miles with the locomotive riding like a Pullman car!

A very beautiful train brought the President of France and his wife from Dover, Marine, to London, Victoria, in 1950. Carrying the royal train headcode, Class MN 3-cylinder 4-6-2 No 35019 *French Line CGT* was resplendent in the then fashionable royal blue of British Railways with the inside of the cab painted white.

Ten minutes before train-time, the railway at Shakespeare Cliff was obscured by thick sea mist. Then, the sun broke through, and I obtained my best 'pictorial' train photograph.

The train passed and, after a difficult climb, I arrived hot and dusty at the cliff top to be confronted by about 200 assorted women who surged forward, thrusting bits of paper and pencils at me. Angrily, I demanded what it all meant. Doubt spread over their homely faces and a voice piped up: 'But you *are* Mr Dimbleby, aren't you?'. On my vehement denial, the crowd melted shamefacedly away.

Delaware and Hudson 4-6-2 No 652 Class P-1 is seen here with train No 7 from New York to Montreal (Canada). It was photographed in 1944 approaching Montreal West station. No 652 was one of two Pacifics built in the Colonie shops of the railway in 1929. No 651 was equipped with o.c. Dabeg poppet valves.

The D & H design team was much influenced by European practice and particularly by the work of W. A. Stanier. The result can be seen in the exceptionally clean lines and lack of external pipe work in the design of No 652. The very European smoke deflectors, the recessed headlight and the almost completely Stanier chimney are in strong contrast with the very wide Wootton firebox.

The ultimate in express passenger locomotive design on the standard gauge New South Wales Railways was thirty Pacifics of Class C.38. The first five were streamlined and were outshopped by Clyde Engineering Company in 1943. During the next five years, thirteen came from the NSW works at Eveleigh and twelve from the Cardiff works. They were very successful and well loved locomotives but, despite their massive appearance, the tractive effort was only 36,200lb and the coupled wheel diameter 69in. They had hand-fired Belpaire boilers.

The trans-Continental standard gauge railway between Perth, WA and Sydney, NSW was completed in 1970 and is operated by diesel locomotives. During September 1970, however, the whole of the 2,461-mile railway was traversed in each direction by the steam-hauled Western Endeavour Express organised by the Rail Transport Museum. Two Class C.38 Pacifics worked the train, No 3801 streamlined and No 3813 without streamlining. The train was the object of great interest throughout Australia and I had the great good fortune to be able to photograph it at Penrith, thirty-four miles from Sydney as it neared the end of its historic journey.

The Reading Railway ran four named streamline trains in each direction each week-day between Jersey City, NJ and Philadelphia, PA. The Crusader made two journeys daily, covering the 90.2 miles in 98 minutes with four intermediate stops. Each train consisted of five stainless steel cars including a dining car with cocktail lounge and an observation car.

The locomotives which worked the 'streamliners' were originally of the well-tried Class G-1sa introduced in 1921. They had wide, mechanically-fired fireboxes and 80in coupled wheels. Stainless steel shrouding was built round two of the engines (Nos 117 and 118) and this probably increased maintenance problems while gaining nothing more than a fashionable appearance. These two locomotives were Class G-1sas and No 118 is shown here with the northbound Crusader passing Elizabethport, NJ 'on the advertised' in 1941.

The crack express of the Lehigh Valley Railroad was the Black Diamond which first ran between New York and Buffalo, NY, in 1896. In its later years the New York terminal for the train was the Pennsylvania station and 'Pennsy' electric locomotives handled the train between there and Newark, NJ. Here steam took over and the 436.2 miles to Buffalo were run in 10hr 29min with sixteen intermediate stops. Much of the train was air-conditioned and there was a dining car, parlour and observation cars.

The locomotives were rebuilds of ALCO-built Pacifics of Class K-6 with 77in coupled wheels, outshopped in 1924 and 1926. They were provided with roller bearings for all axles and for big-ends. The driving wheels were of the Boxpok type. The rather phallic streamline shrouding was gaily painted and the locomotives were re-classified K-6-s. No 2097 was photographed at Oak Island Roundhouse, NJ, in 1941 before working the Black Diamond.

The New York Central Hudsons (4-6-4) were among the world's finest express locomotives. ALCO outshopped all but 10 of the 275 built between 1927 (Class J-1a) and 1938 (Class J-3a). Earlier engines had 25 x 28in cylinders, 79in spoked coupled wheels and 225 psi pressure. Later engines had 22½ x 29in cylinders, either Scullin or Boxpok 79in coupled wheels and 275 psi. All had boosters on the trailing trucks and 20, built for Boston & Albany had 72in coupled wheels.

During the 'streamline era' of the mid-thirties, 10 Class J-3a were streamlined for such trains as the Twentieth Century Limited and the Empire State Express. In 1941, I rode No 5447 working the latter train and my photograph shows her at Harmon Roundhouse before we left to go roaring along the Hudson Valley at 85mph with a wide open throttle, 40 per cent cut off and 900 tons of gleaming stainless steel train behind the tender. Truly some of the most magnificent railroading of all time.

New York, New Haven and Hartford 4-6-4 No 1409 was the last of ten Class 1-5 locomotives outshopped by Baldwin in 1937. I photographed it at Southampton Roundhouse, Boston, Mass in 1941 while the ostler was at work with a steam spray gun removing oil and dirt from the aluminium painted centres of the Boxpok coupled wheels.

These locomotives were required to work 830-ton, 12-car trains on the Short Line Route between Boston and New Haven, Conn, running the 156.8 miles in 185 minutes with three intermediate stops. With a full load they were required to average 60mph against a six-mile gradient, ruling at 1 in 140 (0.7 per cent). This they did but left behind them a trail of broken rails and, it was found, that at 75mph the driving wheels were lifting nearly 1in from the track at each revolution! Re-balancing cured the trouble.

The last express locomotives for the 1600mm (5ft 3in)-gauge Victorian Railways in Australia, were seventy Class R 4-6-4s built by North British in 1951-3. Owing to dieselisation, few ran more than 200,000 miles before being withdrawn, the last in 1968.

The Class R locomotives had cast steel engine beds and SCOA-P coupled wheels. All axles ran in roller bearings and maximum axle load was 19.5 tons. The all-welded Belpaire fireboxes each had two thermic syphons and mechanical stokers were fitted to all but two which were oil fired.

Two are still in existence, No 704 is in the Railway Museum at North Williamstown, Melbourne and No 707 is kept at Newport Workshops where it is maintained in running order for special trains.

My photograph shows No 707 on a train of old coaches at Flinders Street Station, Melbourne. Towering above is a gantry of somersault signals.

Heading an eastbound trans-Canada express leaving Montreal West in 1944, was Canadian Pacific 4-6-4 No 2824 Class H-1c. No 2850, Class H-1d, worked the royal train westwards across Canada during the visit of King George VI and Queen Elizabeth in 1939. Consequently, the King granted permission for the class to be known as Royal Hudsons and, thereafter, coronets were carried on the leading ends of the running plates.

CPR introduced Hudsons in 1929 but the forty domeless, streamlined engines were built in 1937 and 1939. Five, Class H-1d, had boosters on the trailing trucks. The Royal Hudsons were excellent machines and rode beautifully. I made several footplate journeys on them between Montreal and Quebec. A trans-Canada footplate pass was offered but, unfortunately, my naval duties prevented acceptance.

In the development of the steam locomotive, the last two decades before World War II were the most interesting. Advances in metallurgy coupled with good design reduced maintenance and improved availability.

Engineers still tried to improve thermal and overall efficiency: turbine drives and very high boiler pressures with compound cylinders seemed to be the most promising.

On the LNER, in 1929 appeared Gresley's 4-cylinder compound 4-6-4 No 10000 with a 5-drum Yarrow water-tube boiler and 450psi pressure. In service, leaking tubes and difficulty in keeping the fire spaces and smokebox airtight, prevented the engine from steaming reliably. In 1937 it was rebuilt with three simple cylinders and a conventional boiler.

For several years, however, No 10000 ran spasmodically in revenue-earning service and, in 1930, I photographed it working an up East Coast express, passing Craigentinny under clear signals.

Until modernisation really got under way, about six years ago, Spain provided the student of steam locomotive practice with an almost infinite variety of motive power, from 100-year old 0-6-0s (page 23) to the largest and most advanced types in Europe (page 70). This panorama was probably equalled only in India.

I spent much time on the Spanish National Railways System (RENFE), often in the summer heat when the sulphurous smells of locomotive depots and the sharing of cold rough wine with the men on a fiendishly hot footplate, remain most vivid memories.

It was quite usual to see old locomotives hauling trains of modern stock, often over some of the roughest track in Europe. No 040-2040, an 0-8-0 built for the Madrid, Alicante & Zaragoza Railway by Parent-Schaken in 1863, was photographed near Torrelano ninety-nine years later while working a train of modern surburban coaches between Alicante and Murcia.

The New York, New Haven and Hartford Railroad has a large freight classification yard at Cedar Hill, Conn, not far from New Haven. In 1941, one of the locomotives working the hump in the yard was this three-cylinder 0-8-0 No 3605 of Class Y-4 built by ALCO in 1924.

Apart from articulated designs, multicylinder locomotives never found favour in North America and the most important 3-cylinder engines were ninety large 4-12-2s for Union Pacific.

In addition to their 0-8-0s, New Haven also had some 3-cylinder 4-8-2s. All the 3-cylinder engines had conjugated valve gear for the middle piston valve, the drive being taken from the leading ends of the piston valve rods as in the British LNE Gresley Pacifics.

During the changeover from 3-phase ac electrification to 3,000 volts dc, many strange combinations of motive power were seen on the Italian State Railways (FS) in Northern Italy. Shown here in 1963, leaving Turin, PN, under the 3-phase 'overhead' are two Franco Crosti 2-8-0s hauling a 'dead' dc electric locomotive and an express for Aosta. The steam locomotives were Group 743 Nos 318 and 326. The electric locomotive of Group 428 would work the train when the dc 'overhead' was reached.

To reduce coal consumption, many FS locomotives were fitted with Franco-Crosti boilers. Flue gases and exhaust steam were led back from the smokebox, through the tubes of two economisers, to exhaust from two laterally placed chimneys in front of the cab. Any saving in coal was offset by the corrosion caused in the system by the formation of sulphuric acid due to the retardation and cooling of the smokebox gases.

Working a passenger train from Athens to Kiparissia in 1958 was this metre-gauge oil-burning 2-8-0 No E 725 of the Piraeus-Athens-Peloponnesus Railway (SPAP). It was built by Henschel in 1936.

I found SPAP a most attractive and interesting railway which encircles the Peloponnese peninsular and includes historic Corinth in its route. The railway crosses the Corinth Canal by a high girder bridge.

In the heyday of steam, SPAP owned some fine locomotives including bar-framed American-built 2-8-2s of 1947 and some elegant Italian engines of the same type which were built by Breda in 1952. Most engines were oil burners.

49

D

This mixed train of the metre-gauge State Railway of Thailand was heading north from Thon Buri, Bangkok to Prachuapk Hirakan when it was photographed, in 1970, at Taling Chan Junction while awaiting the arrival of a southbound express off the single line.

The locomotives were wood-burning 2-8-2s: No 358, on which I was riding, was one of twenty-eight built in Japan in 1936 and 1946 while the train engine was No 437, one of sixty-eight built by Baldwin during World War II and taken over after the war by the Thai Railway from the US Army Transportation Corps.

Although 'State Railway of Thailand' is the official title, nearly all the rolling stock and some locomotives carry the letters RSR — Royal Siam Railway — on one side and the equivalent Thai characters on the other.

South African Railways operate 439 miles of 610mm (2ft)-gauge railway. Some of these narrow gauge lines are in Natal but an important line runs 177 miles from sea level at Port Elizabeth, Cape, up to Avontuur, 2859ft above sea level.

The motive power for the narrow gauge is exclusively steam and the principal locomotive types are 2-8-2 tender engines, first introduced in 1931 and Garratts of the 2-6-0 + 0-6-2 and 2-6-2 + 2-6-2 wheel arrangements. Some of the last named were built in England as recently as 1967.

My photograph is of 2-8-2 No NG 18 Class NG 15 leaving Loerie, 45 miles from Port Elizabeth, with freight for Avontuur in 1968.

Almost all the world's railways, except, notably those in United Kingdom, operated the Mikado or 2-8-2 type. Often it was built as the freight version of a Pacific or 4-6-2 express locomotive, boilers, cylinders and motion being interchangeable. Why railways in Britain did not adopt this useful type has never been satisfactorily explained. True, Gresley designed two 3-cylinder 2-8-2s which were freight versions of his Class A-1 Pacific but which were regarded as being too powerful and too long for the sidings! He also put into service five others with 74in coupled wheels which, as express locomotives in Scotland, were decidedly unpopular.

Of the many Mikados on which I have travelled, none impressed me more than the husky Jersey Central engines of Class M-2s, built at the Brooks Works of ALCO in 1922. I took this picture of No 876 at Communipaw, NJ in 1941 before travelling on her for nearly 200 miles, working fast freight.

This is one of my favourite railway photographs. It shows Hungarian State Railways (MAV) 4-8-0 No 424.010 leaving Budapest East Station with the Simplon-Orient Express in 1929.

The first twenty-six engines of Class 424 were outshopped in 1924 and a further 190 were added between 1929 and 1944. Others, built after World War II, went to China, Czechoslovakia, Jugoslavia and Russia. Some are still in service and, as always, are very highly regarded by all enginemen.

They are mixed traffic engines and are excellent vehicles, despite the necessity for the high-pitched boiler which enables the wide grate to be accommodated above the third and fourth pairs of coupled wheels. All of the surviving MAV engines now have the Ister double exhaust system.

Turkey is a fascinating country in many ways and, especially, its railways are of great interest, revealing as they do, so much of European history and of the balance-of-power-game played out by Britain, Germany and France in the early years of this century.

There is also a very long tradition of high skills and conscientious work among the railwaymen of the Turkish State Railways (TCDD) who are most interesting and pleasant people.

My last visit to Turkey was in 1958 and among the photographs I took was this of a former main line express locomotive, 4-8-0 No 46010 built by Henschel in 1926, working a Tuzla-Haydarpasa local train leaving Suadiye. These rather ponderous machines also worked trains on the Haydarpasa surburban services often travelling tender-first.

During 1954, my friend the late Hugh le Fleming and I were guests of the Norwegian State Railways (NSB) and of the Danish State Railways (DSB). In each country a comprehensive series of interesting footplate trips was arranged of which one of the highlights was the journey in each direction between Oslo and Bergen.

The locomotives of Class 31b were built specially for the Bergen Line during 1921-6. They were 4-cylinder compounds with an axle load of only 14 tonnes. My photograph, taken at Finse, shows No 419 with Hugh on the footplate.

Even in the Spring, we were in a world of snow and ice and for the first time I experienced the shock of a locomotive with a snow plough, crashing through a large drift. Snow fences and long snow sheds are commonplace on this line which is now electrified.

After World War II, the Czechoslovakian State Railways (CSD) evolved some of the world's most advanced steam locomotives. In many of these the influence of Chapelon was apparent but it was also evident that in the design of frames and of fireboxes, much notice had been taken of the best American practice. So, 4-8-2 No 475.1139, photographed at Breclav in 1967, had excellently designed cylinders with long travel piston valves and direct steam passages, double Kylchap exhaust and an all-welded boiler. The welded steel firebox had a combustion chamber, one thermic syphon and two arch tubes.

All the 147 locomotives of this mixed traffic design had mechanical stokers (though the earliest engines were originally hand-fired) and many had roller bearings for all axles and for the motion. They were built by Skoda during 1947-50.

No 429, one of fifty-two elegant, oil-burning 4-8-2s of the Florida, East Coast Railway, was at the head-end of the South Wind Express from Chicago when I took this photograph at Miami, Flo, FEC Station in 1944. Built by ALCO in 1924 and 1926, the 400 Class had 73 in coupled wheels and were well-liked for their free running and good riding.

FEC was founded and developed by Henry M. Flagler who saw, in Florida, the ideal country for holidays and recreation and who developed Miami from a small fishing port to a great winter holiday resort. Flagler is, however, best remembered as being responsible for the construction of the 156-mile extension to Key West. Numerous keys, or small islands, were connected by concrete bridges the largest of which was seven miles long. The 'railroad that went to sea' took twelve years to build, being completed in 1916 and it enabled Havana, Cuba to be reached in under two days from New York.

In 1935 a violent hurricane and tidal wave destroyed the railway and a passenger train on the line, causing great loss of life. The bridges, however, were not destroyed and, in 1944, I travelled to Key West along the highway which was built over the route of the railway.

The French National Railways Society, (SNCF) owned more compound locomotives than any other of the world's railways.

Introduced in 1925, the first 4-8-2 locomotive in Europe was a Belpaire-boilered, 4-cylinder de Glehn-du Bousquet compound for the Chemin de Fer de l'Est (Eastern Railway). After prototype trials lasting four years, forty more were built for the Est in 1929-31 and these were followed by forty-nine for the Etat who, however, found them unsatisfactory and sold them to the Est. They were powerful and free-steaming machines which appeared to ride excellently but which were very heavy on the track and their speed was limited to 69mph.

Shown here is one of the Est engines, SNCF No 241 A 21 leaving Bar-le-Duc with a semi-fast train for Paris in 1950. On the right is a 4-cylinder compound 4-6-0 working a freight train.

Canadian National 4-8-2 No 6008 Class U-1-a leaving the train shed at Halifax with an evening train for Sidney NS in 1944. This was one of the first batch of Class U-1 built in 1923. The final batch appeared twenty-one years later (Class U-1-f) and brought the total of these 4-8-2s up to eighty. While cylinder (26 x 30in) and coupled wheel (73in) dimensions were unaltered, later engines had the boiler pressure increased from 210psi of the earlier engines to 250psi and their appearance was similar to that of the 4-8-4s.

Clearly seen at the corner of the front pilot beam is the push-pole socket. A steel rod (push-pole) can be inserted therein and in the corresponding socket of a vehicle on an adjacent track. This vehicle can then be moved by the locomotive without the need of its being on the same track.

With a long freight for Cookhouse, SAR 4-8-2 No 3111, Class 15F, was photographed as it drifted towards a home signal at danger at Swartkops Junction in 1968.

Class 15F forms the largest group of main line locomotives on SAR; 255 were built in Germany and Britain during 1938-48. They have piston valves, so differing from the forty-four engines, Class 15E, built during 1935-37 with r.c. poppet valves.

Many Class 15F have mechanical stokers and some, like No 3111, work through long single-bore tunnels on the heavy grades between Port Elizabeth and Cookhouse. These have steam operated smoke deflectors. Two small steam cylinders on the smokebox front operate a plate which slides 6in above the chimney. The exhaust strikes the plate and is deflected into a trough and thence over the top of the cab. At least, that is the idea: enginemen say it makes conditions in the cab worse and it is seldom used.

With clouds of black smoke indicative of soft coal, South African Railways 4-8-2 No 2398, Class 19D and 4-6-2 No 878, Class 16DA were photographed leaving Glen, Orange Free State, in 1968.

Class 19D were introduced in 1937 as branch line engines with a 13.4-ton axle load. They were soon, however, used on a wide range of duties.

Five Class 16DA with wide fireboxes having 60sq ft of grate, were built in 1930 for main line express trains but, those surviving, are relegated to secondary duties.

The signals on the left of the picture are of interest. The upper arm with pointed end, is peculiar to SAR and is an outer home signal, sited 1200ft in advance of the home signal whose aspect it indicates. It may be passed at danger under a stop and proceed rule. The lower arm is a distant which indicates the condition of the section further ahead.

Leaving Lachine, Que, with a westbound freight, Canadian National 4-8-4 No 6244, Class U-2-h was photographed in 1944. Three hundred and eleven of these magnificent Northerns of Class U-2 were built for CNR in batches between 1927 (U-2-a) and 1944 (U-2-h). There were differences between batches; later engines had cast steel engine beds and Boxpok coupled wheels; Class U-2-h had exhaust steam injectors in place of feed water pumps. All had 73in coupled wheels, 25½ x 30in cylinders and 250psi boiler pressure.

I rode on the footplate of several of these fine locomotives. Most vividly remembered is a 282-mile trip on No 6211 working the 1011-ton Ocean Limited Express (Montreal-Halifax) on part of its 842-mile journey. With the mechanical stoker maintaining full boiler pressure, mile after mile was reeled off at 55mph with full regulator and 40 per cent cut-off. The noise of the exhaust was quite thrilling.

Canadian National 4-8-4 No 6400, Class U-4-a was the first of eleven streamlined Northerns outshopped between 1936 and 1938. These were express-engine versions of the Class U-2 (page 62) and the Boxpok coupled wheels were 75 in diameter. Slightly smaller cylinders were used in view of the increase in boiler pressure from 250 to 275 psi. The reason for the streamlining of these engines was mainly to eliminate the drifting down of smoke and steam over the cab which obscured the enginemen's view. The louvres at the front of the casing can be seen in the photograph which was taken in 1944 at the Union Station, Toronto. No 6400 was chosen to work the royal train over much of the CNR system during the memorable and important visit of King George VI and Queen Elizabeth to the United States and Canada in 1939.

The sun blazed vertically down on this busy scene on the South African Railways at Oranje Rivier, Cape with the arrival of the Kimberley-Cape Town express. No 3449 was one of fifty 4-8-4s, Class 25 NC (non condensing) which were built in 1953 and which were identical, mechanically, with the ninety 4-8-4s of Class 25 with Henschel condensing tenders. They are the world's most powerful 1067mm-gauge non-articulated steam locomotives. The tractive effort (85 per cent) is 51,400lb and mechanical stokers feed their 70sq ft of grate. They have roller bearings for all axles and side-rod bearings.

Opposite, seen from above, is one of the Henschel condensing tenders of Class 25.

Exhaust steam from the cylinders first passes to a turbine which drives a fan blower in the smokebox and which replaces the usual draft from a blast-pipe. From the blower turbine, the steam is led along the side of the engine, through a grease separator to another turbine in the tender which drives five air intake fans (seen here) through a line shaft and bevel gearing. Finally the steam passes to banks of condenser elements mounted on both sides of the tender and condensate is collected in a tank below the tender frame to be used over again. A saving of 85 per cent in feed water is achieved and the only difficulty is the corrosion damage caused to blower fan blades in the smokebox by char from the fire.

The Richmond, Fredericksburg and Potomac Railroad operates only 113½ route miles of railway but provides an essential link between the complex of lines to the north and those serving the south of the United States eastern seaboard. The northern terminal is Washington DC (the Potomac [river] in the title) where connection is made with four major railroads while, at Richmond Va, four railroads serving the south and south west depend largely on RF & P for their traffic.

To operate RF & P's heavy and fast transit traffic, Baldwin built twenty-seven massive 4-8-4 stoker-fired locomotives in four batches between 1937 and 1945. They had Boxpok coupled wheels and a tractive effort of 62,800lb. Unusually, the engines were named, the first five after confederate generals and the others after Virginian governors and statesmen. No 555 *General J E Johnston* was photographed in 1944 at Potomac Yard Roundhouse after working fast freight from Richmond, Va.

Some of the richest iron ore in the world is found in the north of Sweden within the Arctic Circle. Serving the area is a single line railway which connects Luleå on the Gulf of Finland with the Norwegian port of Narvik from whence the ore is shipped.

To operate heavy trains over the 1 in 100 (1 per cent) gradients in the extremely severe winter conditions, both the Norwegian and the Swedish State Railways introduced powerful 0-10-0 locomotives. The Norwegian engines entered service in 1913 but the Swedish State Railways (SJ) had their Class R engines in 1909.

The railway was electrified during 1915-23 and then, the Norwegian engines, rebuilt as 2-10-0 to reduce their 16.2 tonne axle-load to 15 tonnes, went to the Oslo-Bergen line. The SJ engines, with a 17-tonne axle were not rebuilt but worked mineral traffic between Gavle and Falun where I photographed No 977 in 1961.

While travelling north on a Pacific of the Finnish State Railways (VR) near Kausala in 1961, I saw in the distance a freight train speeding southwards and leaving behind a dense cloud of black smoke. Balancing myself against the rather wild antics of the Pacific's footplate, I managed to get this picture of 2-10-0 Class Tr 2 No 1306. Unfortunately the smoke greatly moderated when we met and some of the drama was lost.

The VR 2-10-0s came from Baldwin in 1946. They were rugged machines with bar frames, two outside cylinders and Walschaerts valve gear. There were four circulating tubes supporting the brick arch in the firebox and all the engines had mechanical stokers. The middle pair of coupled wheels were without flanges.

No 50.522, a 2-10-0 of the German Federal Railway (DB) was photographed while passing Braubach, on the East Bank of the Rhine, as it worked a heavy southbound freight in 1959.

The successful Class 50 locomotives were introduced by the Reichsbahn as a standard type (*Einheitslokomotiven*) before World War II. They first appeared in 1938 but most were built after Germany entered the war. To economise in materials and labour, many were modified and these, like No 50.522, were Class 50 UK (*Uberkriegsloko-motiven*); they could be recognised by their shortened running plates which reached only to the back ends of the cylinders.

In 1942, the design was again altered by the introduction of all-welded steel boilers and the fabrication of many parts. These engines were Class 52, the famous *Kriegslokomotiven*; many thousands were built. In Classes 50 and 52, the axle load was only 15.2 tonnes.

Prominent among the giants of European steam were the twenty-two 3-cylinder 2-10-2 heavy freight locomotives of the Spanish National Railways, (RENFE) which were built by Maquinista during 1942-5 to a Norte (Northern Railway) design but which entered service after the formation of RENFE in 1941. They had Lentz o.c. poppet valves, ACFI feed water pumps and heaters, double Kylchap exhausts and mechanical stokers, (except for seven which were oil burners).

After the electrification of the line from the Ponferrada coal mines to La Coruña, these engines worked heavy coal trains from León and it was on these duties that I travelled on them to make recordings for the BBC in 1960. Also, I made this picture of No 151-3109 on a coal train near Palencia.

In 1932 the Paris, Lyons and Mediterranean Railway (PLM) put into service ten large 4-cylinder compound freight locomotives. The drive was divided, the low pressure cylinders driving the first two coupled axles and the high pressure cylinders, the last three. The two groups of coupled wheels were synchronised by inside coupling rods between the second and third axles, both of which were cranked. Both high pressure and low pressure cylinders had Dabeg r.c. poppet valves, the drive for the valves on each side of the engine being taken from a return crank on the second coupled wheels on each side.

After the formation of SNCF in 1938, these engines went to the Est (Eastern) Region to work the heavy international coal and iron ore trains over the steeply graded lines of the Basin of Briey, and No 151 A 3 was photographed at Audun-le-Roman in 1950.

The combined tractive effort (at 85 per cent boiler pressure) of these two locomotives of the Bulgarian State Railways (BDZ) was 106,700lb. No 11.01, a 3-cylinder 4-10-0 and No 01.20, a 2-cylinder 2-8-2, were at the head-end of the Jugoslavia Express which they had worked over the steeply graded line from Sofia to the Bulgaria-Jugoslavia frontier station of Dragomen where the photograph was taken on a dull morning in 1964.

Twenty-two 3-cylinder 4-10-0s were supplied to BDZ by German builders during 1941-3 in the middle of a world war! They were the only multicylinder 4-10-0s ever built: even 2-cylinder 4-10-0s were very rare, the famous *El Gobernador* of the Central Pacific Railroad of America being the prototype. This locomotive was built in 1884 and it is possible that one or two examples of the type were built for other American railroads.

Indonesian State Railways (PNKA) oil-fired 2-6-2T No C24 03 was photographed in 1970 while working on the south to north line between Jogjakarta and Ambarawa in Java. This 1067mm (3ft 6in)-gauge line runs for many miles beside the main road and, to obtain this photograph, the train was chased and overtaken by our mini bus to the obvious amazement of the occupants of the horse and trap who stopped to watch the fun!

Further north, the line is very steeply graded with a rack section of nearly four miles before Ambarawa (page 89). These 2-6-2 Tank locomotives were built by Werkspoor in Amsterdam in 1908 and are of particular interest as they were among the first locomotives in the world to be fitted with Schmidt superheaters. Indeed, with their piston valves and smart modern appearance it is difficult to realise that they are more than sixty years old.

The State Railways of Bulgaria (BDZ) operated the largest non-articulated tank locomotives in the world. They were required to work the very heavy coal traffic over the heavily graded route between the mines in the Pernik area and the marshalling yards at Sofia though they were also used for heavy hauls in other areas.

My photograph, taken in 1964 near Vladaya, shows 2-12-4T No 46.12 working coal empties towards Pernik. This locomotive was one of twelve outshopped by Cegielski in Poland in 1931 and was a 2-cylinder simple.

In 1943 (in the middle of a world war) Schwartzkopff of Berlin supplied eight 3-cylinder 2-12-4T which, though more elegant in appearance than were the 2-cylinder machines, were never liked as much by the men.

The 0-8-4 Tank locomotives of the 1676mm (5ft 6in)-gauge Great Indian Peninsular Railway were built in several batches, No 41 of Class Y/3 seen here at Hope Hall Shed, Byculla, in 1940, being one of 16 supplied by North British in 1912.

These heavy and powerful locomotives were required for banking purposes on the 41 miles of the Western Ghat inclines on the main line between Bombay and points east. The ruling gradient on the Ghats is 1 in 37 (2.7 per cent).

The original Y Class locomotives were introduced in 1906 and were saturated 2-8-4T. In order to increase the adhesive weight, the leading pony truck was removed experimentally on two of these engines and subsequent batches were built as 0-8-4T.

The railway over the Ghats and beyond has been electrified since 1932 and the banking engines were, thereafter, used for shunting in various freight yards, some going to the East Indian Railway.

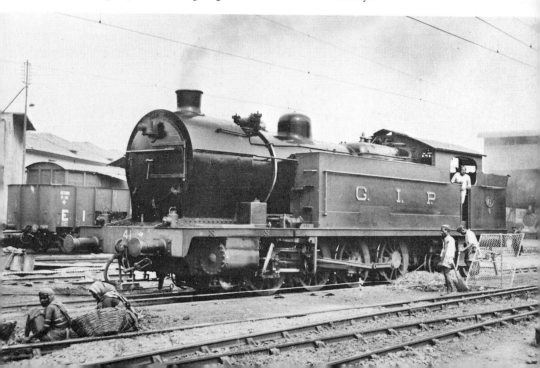

Réseau Breton was the last of four narrow-gauge railways in Brittany. It was part of the State Railways (Chemins de Fer de l'Etat) until being absorbed into SNCF in 1938.

The 243-mile, metre-gauge system was well maintained but increasing competition from road transport forced its closure in 1967 after eighty years of service.

During 1964, I saw much of the Réseau Breton. Most passenger services were then operated by diesel-mechanical railcars though some trains were hauled by 4-6-0T of which twelve were in service. Freight trains were worked by nine saturated Mallet compound 0-6-6-0T, No 41 of which had been acquired in 1953 and eight, Nos E410-E417, were built for the railway during 1914-16. All had slide valves and weighed 54.6 tonnes. They could haul 320-tonne trains up a 1 in 50 (2 per cent) gradient at 12mph.

My photograph shows No E 416 passing Carnoët Locarn with a Carhaix-Guingamp van train.

The Portuguese Railway Company (CP) operates a considerable mileage of metre-gauge lines, the most important being those of the former Minho e Douro Railway (MD) to the north and east of Oporto. This company also had a number of feeder lines running down the valleys to the Douro, 1665mm (5ft 5 9/16in)-gauge, main line.

Among a considerable number of metre-gauge Mallet compound tank locomotives taken into CP stock were sixteen built by Henschel and introduced on the MD in 1911. These are of the unusual 2-4-6-0T wheel arrangement and, although they are not superheated, piston valves are provided for all four cylinders.

Photographed in 1960 at the head of a mixed train leaving Regua for Chaves was No E 203 ('E' indicates narrow gauge). On the left, is a broad gauge, outside cylinder, 0-6-0 No 23 built by Beyer Peacock in 1875.

Working on the hump in Potomac Yard, Alexandria, Va, in 1944 was this 2-6-6-2 Mallet compound of the Chesapeake and Ohio Railway. No 1411 of Class H-4 was outshopped in 1917 by ALCO who built 150 of the class. The design was a development of C & O's first Mallets of 1910, Class H-1. Class H-4 had piston valves for the high pressure cylinders and balanced slide valves above the low pressure cylinders. All the later compound Mallets had piston valves for all four cylinders and some of Class H-4 were rebuilt with four high pressure cylinders.

(While photographing this locomotive, I was detained by two members of the FBI. They acted very quickly and surprisingly quietly and insisted on my accompanying them to the District Office. Fortunately my credentials were in order, and I was later able to continue my photography).

Among the best looking of all the simple Mallet locomotives in the USA, were the Delaware and Hudson 4-6-6-4s of Class J-95. No 1500 was built by ALCO in 1940 and I photographed her working northbound freight past Schenectady (Mohawk), NY, in 1941. During the period 1940-6 a total of forty of these fine locomotives were built.

Through the courtesy of the late George Edmonds, Motive Power Superintendent, I was able to make two journeys on the footplates of these engines — an unforgettable experience. With 69in coupled wheels they were capable of a good turn of speed while a tractive effort of 94,000lb was testimony of their elegant power.

Indonesian State Railways (PNKA) oil-burning 2-6-6-0 Mallet compound No CC50 18, was photographed at Sidotopo MPD, Surabaya in 1970. During 1927-8 fourteen of these locomotives were built for the Java State Railways by Werkspoor and sixteen, including No CC50 18 by Swiss Locomotive Company. Developing some 1300 ihp, these were among the most powerful locomotives ever designed for 1067mm (3ft 6in) gauge and most of them still remain to work freight and secondary passenger trains. Piston valves were provided for both high pressure and low pressure cylinders; the tenders were of characteristic Dutch design. The bat-shaped objects seen on the front of the smokebox, house coloured head code discs which can be moved across the headlights to indicate the class of train being worked.

The firm of Hartmann of Chemnitz built a number of Meyer articulated locomotives among which were fifteen standard gauge 0-4-4-0T out-shopped between 1910 and 1914 for the Saxon State Railways as their Class I TV. They worked a branch line near Dresden on which there were steep gradients and severe curves.

No 98.009 was the last of these engines in service on DR. It was photographed at Dresden, Alstadt, in 1967.

The Meyer principle of articulation differs from that of the Mallet in that both power units are in bogies to which the draw and buffing gear are attached, whereas in the Mallet, the high pressure unit is in the main frame and only the forward, low pressure unit, is in a bogie. In the Meyer, the cylinders are back to back, the low pressure cylinders being behind the high pressure, the reverse of the Mallet design.

The 600mm (1ft 11½in)-gauge Festiniog Railway was one of several British railways to use double Fairlie articulated locomotives in the latter part of last century. It is, however, alone in having such locomotives still in service.

My photograph shows 0-4-4-0T No 10 *Merddin Emrys* with a train for Portmadoc at Blaenau Festiniog in 1939. This locomotive was built in the Company's works at Boston Lodge in 1879.

The double Fairlie locomotive has a double boiler with two inner fireboxes separated by a water leg but having a common wrapper plate and outer casing. There are two smokeboxes — one at each end of the locomotive. The boiler is carried on a girder frame extending the whole length of the locomotive and supported by two powered bogies which are pivotted at their centres but which are stabilised by swing links connecting each bogie frame to the main frame of the locomotive.

South African Railways 2-6-2 + 2-6-2 Garratt locomotive No 2259, Class GDA, was working a northbound passenger train from Durban (Natal) to Empangeni when it was photographed passing a southbound freight headed by 4-8-2 + 2-8-4 No 4012, Class GEA near Zinkwazi in 1968.

Five Class GDA were built by Linke Hoffman in 1929 for branch lines in the Cape but they had many faults and, ultimately, went to Durban where they worked light passenger and freight trains on the North Coast line.

Class GEA were among the most successful of all SAR Garratts and fifty came from Beyer Peacock in 1946-7. With more than 51sq ft of grate they were hand-fired but when I travelled on No 4048 working a heavy express train over the 1 in 40 (2.5 per cent) gradients of the Montague Pass, firing was well within the capabilities of one fireman.

Photographed in 1970 leaving Gosford, NSW with freight for Newcastle was this enormous standard gauge 4-8-4 + 4-8-4 Garratt of the New South Wales Railways. No 6009 was one of fifty Class AD.60 built by Beyer Peacock in 1952. These were some of the largest Garratts ever built and they were the largest and most powerful locomotives in Australia.

With a tractive effort of 59,560lb and 55in coupled wheels their work was almost entirely on the heavy freight trains common to the densely industrialised area north of Sydney. The engines were designed to burn coal from the area of Newcastle and they had mechanical stokers to feed their 63.4sq ft of grate.

Several were still hard at work during the final days of steam in Australia but, in 1970, they had obviously seen better days and I was lucky to be able to photograph them.

The 1067mm (3ft 6in)-gauge South African Railways were among the largest users of Garratt articulated locomotives in the world and many of these powerful machines are still at work. The largest of all the SAR Garratts were the Class GL 4-8-2 + 2-8-4, the first two of which went into service in 1929 and were followed by six more in 1930. They were built for the steeply graded Durban-Johannesburg line but when electrification of this line was completed in 1938, the GLs were transferred to Glencoe to work heavy coal trains between there and Vryheid. These great locomotives ended their days working from Stanger, north of Durban, Natal and my 1968 photograph shows No 2351 *Princess Alice* working a northbound freight near Zinkwazi. It is possible that this locomotive will be preserved.

This RENFE express from Barcelona to Valencia was photographed leaving Salou in 1962. Two oil-burning 4-6-2 + 2-6-4 Garratts Nos 462^{F}0402 and 0404 provided ample motive power as well as plenty of pollution!

Six of these great locomotives were built for the Central of Aragón Railways by Euskalduna in 1930 for working over the mountainous route between Valencia and Calatayud. When, in 1941, they came into RENFE stock they were sent to work between Tarragona and Valencia, the non-electrified part of the busy Barcelona-Valencia route.

With 69in coupled wheels, these Garratts were classified as express locomotives and it was while riding on No 462^{F}0402 in 1961 that I travelled at a sustained 66mph for 4½ miles, the first and only time I have ever exceeded 60mph on an articulated locomotive.

The Snowdon Mountain Railway, Britain's only rack railway, is laid to the 800mm (2ft 7½in) gauge and extends for 4 5/8 miles from Llanberis to Snowdon summit. Nowhere is the line level, the easiest gradient being 1 in 50 (2 per cent) and the steepest 1 in 5.5 (18.2 per cent). The line is 'pure rack', operated on the Abt system.

The seven steam locomotives were built by Swiss Locomotive Works, four in 1895-6 and three with superheaters, in 1922-3. All have outside cylinders driving the rack pinions through rocking levers and connecting rods. They may loosely be described as 0-4-2T but there is no adhesion drive and all are carrying wheels only.

My photograph of No 6 *Padarn* (built 1922) was taken during several happy days spent on SMR and its locomotives when, in 1963, I was obtaining material for the first edition of my book on the railway.

Austrian Federal Railways (ÖBB) operate a single line railway connecting iron-ore workings at Eisenerz, Styria, with blast furnaces at Donawitz. On either side of the summit at Prabichl are long sections with ruling gradients of 1 in 14 (7 per cent) operated on the Abt rack system.

Three types of rack and adhesion tank locomotives worked on the line: eighteen 0-6-2T, three 0-12-0T and two 2-12-2T. All had four high pressure cylinders, the steeply inclined inside pair driving the rack pinions independently of two outside cylinders driving the adhesion wheels. All had counter-pressure braking and, on ore trains, they worked in pairs, one hauling and one banking. Several 0-6-2T are still at work.

No 197.301, an 0-12-0T designed by Gölsdorf and built by Floridsdorf in 1912, was photographed in 1956 while banking a train of ore wagons. It had a Giesl ejector and behind the chimney are the silencers for the counter-pressure brake exhaust.

On the Jogjakarta-Semarang line of the Indonesian State Railways in Java, south of Ambarawa is a section of line operated on the Abt rack system. Compared with other rack railways, the ruling gradient of 1 in 8 (12.5 per cent) is not severe. Stationed at Ambarawa are five wood-burning 4-cylinder compound 0-4-2T rack and adhesion locomotives built by Esslingen in 1905. No B25 03 was photographed at Ambarawa in 1970.

The adhesion wheels are driven by the high pressure cylinders which exhaust direct to atmosphere unless the locomotive is on the rack when the exhaust is turned into the low pressure cylinders which drive the rack pinions through reduction gearing. As the speed of the low pressure pinions is thus nearly double that of the high pressure pistons, the size of low pressure and high pressure cylinders is identical. These locomotives have parallel boilers; the gradient is not severe enough to warrant the usual forward inclination of the boiler, so often a necessary feature of rack locomotive design.

The day's journey between Sarajevo and Dubrovnik on the 760mm-gauge lines of the Jugoslav Railways (JZ) was one of the most interesting of all my travels on railways. A standard gauge electrified line has now been completed between Sarajevo and Mostar so the most fascinating part of the narrow gauge line is no more

The steeply graded section of the 760mm-gauge line between Bradina and Konjic was operated on the Abt rack system by thirty-eight 0-6-0 rack and adhesion locomotives with Stütz articulated tenders. Outside cylinders drove the adhesion wheels and two, steeply inclined, inside cylinders drove the rack pinions. All cylinders took steam from the boiler and were not compounded, the rack unit having separate controls. The locomotives had counter-pressure braking and Joy valve gear.

No 97.024 was photographed at Bradina in 1966. In the background is one of the well-known 0-8-2 mixed traffic engines.

In the Austrian Tyrol is the metre-gauge, Riggenbach rack, Achenseebahn which starts from Jenbach, 1738ft above sea level and extends 2½ miles to Eben, 3182ft, against a ruling gradient of 1 in 6¼ (16 per cent). Here the rack ends and the locomotive which has pushed one or two passenger cars up to Eben station, now runs round and, coupling on the front, hauls its train by adhesion only over a further 1.9 miles of slightly falling gradients, to the lakeside terminus at Achensee. Returning, the locomotive, bunker first, hauls its train to Eben where the rack is engaged for the descent to Jenbach.

The line is worked by three 2-cylinder 0-4-0T locomotives built by Floridsdorf in 1889. The cylinders drive a layshaft on which gear wheels drive two rack pinions and also, through another transverse shaft and side rods, the four adhesion wheels. The valve gear is Joy's.

Seen here, soon after arriving at Achensee, is No 3 at the head of its one-coach train. Also visible is the back of another train about to leave for Jenbach.

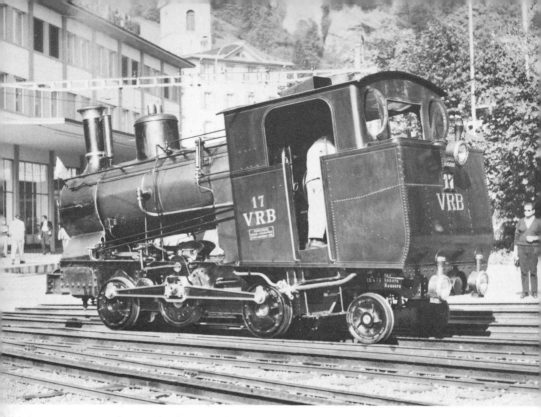

The standard-gauge Vitznau Rigi-Bahn is an electrified mountain railway in Switzerland which, in 1971, celebrated its centenary. The railway still owns two superheated 0-4-2T steam locomotives, Nos 16 and 17 built by SLM in 1923 and 1925 respectively and, during the summer of 1971, a steam-operated train was run each workday between Vitznau and Rigi-Kaltbad. My photograph shows No 17 leaving the shed at Vitznau.

The rack system is Riggenbach and the locomotives are 'pure rack' although the geared drive from the inside cylinders through side-rods to the rack pinions, also drives the adhesion wheels. As built, the rack pinions only were driven but, in 1934, the engines were rebuilt and the driven wheel centres were fixed to the tyres of the four leading wheels. The boiler is inclined forward to ensure even coverage of tubes and firebox when the engine is on the mountain.

Societies for the preservation of steam locomotives have become a recognised part of the railway scene in Britain and other countries during recent years. One such successful enterprise is the Sittingbourne & Kemsley Light Railway, a 762mm (2ft 6in)-gauge line in Kent. Originally an industrial line, it ran between the Bowater Lloyd paper mill at Sittingbourne and the company's Ridham Dock on the Swale. The present extent of the line is from Sittingbourne to Kemsley only.

The railway, together with six locomotives, rolling stock and equipment, was handed over to the Locomotive Club of Great Britain in October 1969 for a nominal rental and the club has operated the line, mainly during summer week-ends, ever since.

Shown in my photograph, taken at Kemsley Terminal, is *Premier* with a train for Sittingbourne. This 0-4-2ST was built by Kerr Stuart in 1906.

CAMERAS, MATERIALS, COLLECTIONS

Starting in 1917 with a Box Brownie, I next owned a Butcher folding ¼-plate camera with a Ross f4.5 lens and then, in 1922, came a Dallmeyer ¼-plate reflex with a focal-plane shutter speeded to a nominal 1/1000sec. Concurrently, I used a 6 x 9cm Super Ikonta with a rather soft-focus f3.8 Tessar lens. It was this camera which went to war with me and with which I was, among other things, an official naval photographer.

Since the war, I have worked with many cameras, including a 9 x 12cm VN Press, a Speed Graphic and a 6 x 9cm Zeiss Deckrullo with an f3.5 Tessar, the finest lens I have ever used.

My present most important equipment comprises three 6 x 9cm folding cameras:
- (i) a Selfix-820, purchased in 1947 and still giving first class results: mostly used with 6 x 9cm and 6 x 6cm Agfa CT18 colour films;
- (ii) a Zeiss Super Ikonta with Tessar f3.5 lens;
- (iii) a Voigtlander Bessa II with a very fine Apo-Lanthar f4.5 lens.

I have never owned a miniature camera; the obvious grain-size in big enlargements and the difficulty of doing accurate work on the negative, ruled out 35mm from the start.

Sensitive materials are standardised as much as possible. In the old days, Imperial 'Eclipse Ortho' and Ilford 'Soft Gradation Pan' were my usual plates until the arrival of the much faster Agfa Iso Pan.

After the war, Ilford high speed panchromatic plates and cut-film were used in the speed cameras while Ilford HP-3 (now HP-4) 6 x 9cm roll film has been my choice for the folding cameras. Exposures are usually about 1 stop more than meter-reading and development time is cut to about 75 per cent of standard. Prints are on double-weight glossy Agfa 'Brovira' and are left un-glazed.

I have always had an excellently equipped dark-room but I do not process colour films. Plates and films are dish developed in 50 per cent D-76 at 68°F and are checked visually in green safelight before completion of development.

My collection of about 14,050 prints, most of which are of post-card size, is housed in specially made loose-leaf, slip-in albums. Each print is numbered and titled in micro-type and negatives are filed in individual envelopes numbered to correspond with the print.

In recent years, my output of railway photographs has fallen drastically. This is largely compensated by an increasing interest in the photography of ships; but that is another story!

ACKNOWLEDGEMENTS

It is impossible to mention all those to whom I am indebted.

I never cease to be grateful and I never forget the many railway-men who have helped so much to provide for me a very full and interesting life. To my wife for her most generous help and under-standing during the most difficult times, my gratitude knows no bounds. Without her wonderful, unpaid co-operation, emigration would have been inevitable.

INDEX